Choosing the Good Life

Two Competing Economic Visions

Gerard Francis Lameiro, Ph.D.
Founder and CEO, Lameiro Economics LLC
"America's Citizen-Philosopher"

Published by Lameiro Economics LLC, LameiroEconomicsLLC.com.

ISBN: 978-1-45373-436-0

First Print Edition.

Print Edition printed by CreateSpace, CreateSpace.com.

Print edition copies of this book are available through various
websites and bookstores. If your favorite bookstore does not have this
book in stock, you can always request that they special order one or
more copies for you.

For information on buying books at wholesale prices, resellers can
contact CreateSpace. Please visit CreateSpace.com, click on Contact Us,
and then click on the link for CreateSpace Direct Resellers.

For information on the author or to contact the author, please visit
GerardLameiro.com.

For media interview requests, speaking engagement invitations, or
consulting opportunities for the author, please visit GerardLameiro.com.

Cover and Book Design by MDW Graphics and Type, MDWgraphics.com.

God

Contents

About the Book Series

Dr. Lameiro's Series of Short Economic Books on
Life, Liberty, and the Pursuit of Peace and Prosperity -
Timeless Ideas in Less Time™

Choosing the Good Life: Two Competing Economic Visions is the first in a planned series of easy-to-read books that **empower, inspire, and educate readers** by offering practical and meaningful economic knowledge that directly impacts readers and their lives. As planned, each title in the series will be available in both print and Kindle formats.

Written and published on a schedule of about one or two new books every year, each title in the series is short and to the point, providing useful and timeless ideas in less time. This means you can enjoy reading an entire book completely on an airline flight in a few hours or more leisurely in the comfort of your home in just one evening. Plus, with each book capturing essential ideas and information in fewer print pages, you get pragmatic information fast, without the guilt of never having the time to finish "the other 200 or 300 pages."

This series focuses on freedom, economic growth, peace and prosperity, all from the point of view of individuals and their families. The series deals with how the economy really works and how economic policies impact each and every individual and family. The series also deals with the critical relationships among religion and culture, government, and the economy, and how all of these interact together to create prosperity and peace. Or, if not understood and used appropriately, how all of these factors can result in widespread poverty and strife.

Written by Gerard Francis Lameiro, *America's Citizen-Philosopher*, each book in this planned series brings with it Dr. Lameiro's engaging and award-winning style, his optimistic vision, and his uncanny ability to make the complex very simple.

This is an important, practical, and easy-to-read series of books designed to **empower, inspire, and educate readers**. To learn more about other books in this series as they become available and to read Dr. Lameiro's blog, please visit GerardLameiro.com.

About the Author

Gerard Francis Lameiro is CEO of Lameiro Economics LLC, a company focused on bringing practical economic knowledge about freedom, economic growth, and prosperity to America and to the world. Author of *America's Economic War,* Dr. Lameiro was previously a member of Hewlett-Packard's Strategy and Corporate Development team where he was Director of New Business Ventures for HP worldwide and managed HP's Technology Evaluation Process worldwide. He is the former worldwide President of the Association of Energy Engineers (AEE) and a National Science Foundation Post-Doctoral Fellow. Dr. Lameiro was also an Assistant Professor in Colorado State University's College of Business. Dr. Lameiro, a frequent and popular TV and Talk Radio show guest, has been interviewed on Fox News Channel's *Strategy Room; Live on Sunday Night, It's Bill Cunningham; The Rusty Humphries Show*; and many other shows. For more information on the author, or to contact the author, please visit GerardLameiro.com.

Why You Should Read This Book

Choosing the Good Life: Two Competing Economic Visions shines a bright light on one of the greatest issues of the 21st century. It also tees up one of the most vitally important decisions you will ever make as a citizen. Indeed, this book presents the two distinct and competing economic visions for what constitutes the "Good Life."

These economic visions represent two different economic systems, two different ways of looking at life, and two different ways of living life. In fact, they are based on two opposing philosophies of life.

Today, at the beginning of the 21st century, each economic vision is competing for your mind and fighting for your support. Your choice of economic visions will help to determine whether America and our civilization will grow or decline; whether we will live in prosperity or struggle with poverty; and whether we will live in peace or at war. You have enormous power as a citizen to influence, shape and decide America's future. Truly, your choice and the choices of millions of other citizens will ultimately impact and help to determine which economic vision will become reality in America and in the world.

While this book addresses citizens in America in the early 21st century, its principles and knowledge apply equally well across both time and space. The ideas within *Choosing the Good Life* are appropriate to citizens in other nations today, and likely will be relevant for generations of citizens to come in the future. In that sense, it is a classic book on economic freedom.

Chapter 1

The Social Road

"To follow socialist morality would destroy much of
present humankind and impoverish much of the rest."
F. A. Hayek
(Economist and Nobel Prize Winner)

The Social Road always leads to moral and economic bankruptcy. Yet, many mistakenly believe it will result in the Good Life.

What is the Social Road to the Good Life? Why do so many think it's so good? And, how can they be so wrong without ever realizing it? Let's find the answers to these questions below.

Two Giant Contradictions

It's odd when you think about it. Indeed, it appears to be a giant contradiction. The proponents of the Social Road often use lofty language and claim wonderful intentions. Yet, they need to use large doses of deceit, deception and fear to drag people down the Social Road to moral and economic bankruptcy.

These proponents go by many names and certainly you've heard them many times before – progressives, socialists, communists, Marxists – to mention some of the more popular names used in the last 100 years for those eager to move us down the Social Road. Today, the term progressive is certainly the "in" name for the cheerleaders for the Social Road. That term progressive sounds so very positive and well, just downright progressive. How can anyone be against progress?

The advocates for the Social Road often employ the words of moral philosophers and Church leaders – justice, fairness, equality, and morality. But, the Social Road, while cast as an avenue of good intentions, is a corrupt route and a dark alley to moral disintegration and poverty. Indeed, if you study the Social Road in any depth at all, the

---

yellow caution signs abound on every corner, pop up around every bend, and can't possibly be missed.

If this is true, why do so many people in America, often our best and brightest minds in government, in education, and in the media, believe so emphatically that the Social Road is the best road for America to take to achieve the Good Life? Well, to find the answer to this second giant contradiction, we need to start with their economic vision for the Good Life. Let's look at this economic vision, especially in five important areas of our lives: freedom, jobs, money, lifestyle, and health.

The Social Road – Big Government vs. Your Freedom

The Social Road starts with the notion that the Good Life can best be achieved by a large, powerful, and centralized government that micro-manages its citizens and the intimate details of their lives very closely. The proponents of the Social Road believe that the well educated and elite in society (they are referring to themselves, of course) are smarter than ordinary citizens and know best for everyone else.

It's true. Proponents of the Social Road do acknowledge that big government is often inefficient and ineffective. Yet, progressives forgive big government for all of its many sins because of its noble goals and good intentions that are seldom, if ever, realized. Of course, in going down the Social Road, freedom must of necessity be limited. It's simply not possible to have both empowered citizens and an empowered big government.

Freedom – religious freedom, political freedom, economic freedom, intellectual freedom – and power are inextricably linked together. Freedom implies power. Freedom is power. If big government has the freedom and power to make decisions for its citizens, it's obvious that the citizens no longer hold that same freedom and power. While our Founding Fathers believed power belongs to the people and is ceded to government in small bits and pieces, progressive socialists believe power belongs to big government and is given to the people in small bits and pieces.

If you're curious about why an economic vision limits not only economic freedom, but also religious freedom, political freedom, and intellectual freedom, here's a quick way to understand it.

Progressives and others who advocate going on the Social Road want to create a "socialist utopia" as they define it in their minds. That's the Good Life they seek. To create a socialist utopia, they require an immense amount of power and they must control the economy. In turn, to control the economy, they must limit or eliminate economic freedom. If *you* have economic freedom, *they* lose control. So, they must limit or eliminate your economic freedom.

Now, this is where it gets very interesting. To eliminate economic freedom, they must control the government. To control the government, they must eliminate political freedom. It doesn't stop there. To eliminate political freedom, they must control the culture. And, to control the culture, they must eliminate religious freedom. Culture flows naturally from religious theology and philosophy.

That's why the Social Road involves limiting or eliminating all of our freedoms. It also explains why progressives are so adamantly opposed to the U. S. Constitution that guarantees all of our freedoms, even if they casually indicate their passing support for the Constitution. It also explains why the choice of a Supreme Court nominee is so vitally important. Will that nominee interpret the Constitution as our Founding Fathers originally intended as the ultimate guarantor of our freedom (an Originalist interpretation) or will a Supreme Court nominee re-write the Constitution giving more and more power to big government using a progressive socialist version of jurisprudence?

If you want to understand all of these topics in more detail, I have answered many more related questions in my book, *America's Economic War – Your Freedom, Money and Life.* Among other topics, it explains the Architecture of American Capitalism (how our system is built), American Exceptionalism (why our system is unique and special), and Socialism's Chain of Control (how socialism attempts to control people).

So, for starters, we know that the Social Road means big government and limited freedom for citizens. But, that's just a very high level peek at this economic vision. What are some of the many ways that taking the Social Road impacts our day-to-day lives? Let's start with jobs.

The Social Road and Your Job

The Social Road doesn't lead to substantial job creation in the private sector. That's for sure. To pay for big government, taxes are required and they must be high. In turn, these high taxes impede economic growth and job growth. There is more than ample economic data to illustrate this point. For example, the Harding-Coolidge tax cuts, the post World War II tax cuts, the JFK tax cuts, the Reagan tax cuts, and the Bush tax cuts, spurred economic growth and new job creation. Today's high unemployment rate around 9.5% (as I'm writing this book) goes hand-in-hand with today's high (and apparently still growing) tax burden on the American people.

While high taxes mean fewer jobs are created in the private sector, it can also mean new jobs are created in the public sector. Unfortunately for the economy, public sector jobs are typically a less productive use of our scarce economic resources. In general, money invested in the private sector yields a much higher economic multiplier than money spent by big government. That's why big government stimulus packages typically end without much positive impact on the economy. If you need proof points, look at the many failed stimulus attempts in Japan in the 1990s, or our own stimulus package in 2009. The so-called 2009 stimulus package is widely-acknowledged by economists to have failed.

On the Social Road, you find three different types of jobs. First, there are jobs for the elite. These are very powerful and high-paying jobs for those who are politically-correct, politically-connected, or politically-elected to office. These are the best jobs in a progressive socialist country and carry with them the most power, the highest prestige, and many perks both large and small. Oftentimes, they can lead to some "free" money that results from bribery and corruption. Around the world and even in America, we see corruption not only associated with big government, but also quite rampant. In fact, bribery and corruption are the norm in some places. We can call these Tier 1 jobs. They hold the ultimate power in a progressive socialist country.

Second, on the Social Road, there are Tier 2 jobs for the bureaucrats who keep big government running on a day-to-day basis. They make the rules you and your family must obey. They decide if granny will get the medical procedure she needs to live, or the pill to just numb the pain. They decide not only who lives and dies, but our quality of life as well.

They also collect the taxes and enforce the regulations. They wield day-to-day power in a progressive socialist country.

Tier 2 jobs also include those big government workers who are members of public employee unions. You can expect their pension benefits will be higher than private sector businesses because businesses must control expenses and big government can always raise taxes, or create new taxes, or in a real show of euphemistic creativity, impose a tax and give it a non-tax identity (such as a "special benefit assessment" or even just a plain old "fee").

On the Social Road, Tier 1 and Tier 2 jobs are closely related. Do you know why? It's really very straight forward. Tier 1 elites promise more and more pay and benefits to Tier 2 employees, even when big government doesn't have the resources to cover the bills. In turn, Tier 2 workers are more than happy to vote for Tier 1 elites in the hope of keeping their jobs and realizing an ever-increasing stream of pay, perks, and benefits. This type of comfortable arrangement is one of the reasons why some countries in Europe and some States in the United States are running into severe financial problems these days, even the very real prospects of bankruptcy. Where will the bailouts come from to pay for all the promises of big government elites made to their enabling Tier 2 supporters?

Third, on the Social Road, there are Tier 3 jobs or welfare "jobs." Actually, Tier 3 "jobs" are not jobs at all. They are transfer payments and include such things as welfare payments, unemployment benefits, and other unearned income made from big government to individuals. Some transfer payments go to people unable to work because of medical or personal circumstances. These are necessary at all times in any nation, regardless of the economic vision governing a society. We must always provide help for the truly needy and destitute.

In addition, some transfer payments go to people unable to find work because of the systemic unemployment created by the policies of big government. These are the fault of a nation's choice of an economic vision. In a completely free market, everyone who wants a job can always find it. But, in a progressive socialist country, on-going, structural, high unemployment is necessarily the stark reality that job hunters face. Of course, it's the result of bad economic policies on the Social Road.

While some might disagree with calling transfer payments "jobs," these welfare "jobs" are the rough equivalent of other jobs in that they provide basic sustenance to individuals and allow people to live their lives.

One quick point worth noting. There is also a symbiotic relationship between Tier 1 elites and Tier 3 transfer payment recipients. Like Tier 2 employees, Tier 3 people are most likely glad to vote for Tier 1 elites that promise endless new and increased benefits. What Tier 3 welfare recipient would choose to vote for someone who will only maintain their benefits, or worse yet, try to cut back on welfare payments?

Another important point. The three tier jobs model on the Social Road makes one big assumption. It assumes that there will always be a source of money for Tier 1, Tier 2, and Tier 3 pay, benefits, and transfer payments. From an economic vantage point, free enterprise, free markets, and free trade create capital and wealth, and are a source of tax income for legitimate government needs. Progressive socialist countries – with an ever increasing public sector and an ever decreasing private sector – tend to consume capital and wealth until it's gone. That's why the Social Road always leads to economic bankruptcy. It's not a question of IF a progressive socialist country will go bankrupt. It's only a question of WHEN it will go bankrupt.

Notice, too, on the Social Road, that there's not much incentive for creating new jobs in the private sector. Taxes take away the incentives. Regulations take away the simplicity and add to expenses. There's also not much incentive to work in the private sector with public sector pay and benefits often being much higher, and sometimes, requiring correspondingly less personal effort and responsibility. In addition, as tax burdens increase, the incentive to work decreases. It's human nature for individuals to want to keep their earnings. If the fraction of money you keep declines, your motivation to work will probably decline as well. All these factors put together lead to a shrinking private sector on the Social Road and fewer jobs. That's why unemployment is usually much higher in progressive socialist countries.

Progressives think the three job tiers represent a working foundation for the Good Life, even though there is an enormous loss of personal freedom and Tier 2 pay and benefits as well as Tier 3 transfer payments are unsustainable, without a free and economically strong private sector. Without free enterprise and free markets, progressive socialist countries

Choosing the Good Life

spiral downward toward economic bankruptcy. Just recall the riots in Europe over proposed austerity cuts, cuts that were necessitated by out-of-control welfare state spending. Recall, too, how several European nations are struggling to deal with their big government debt loads and battling to avoid bankruptcy. As this book is being written, the significant economic problems with European welfare state socialism are essentially unresolved.

To sum up jobs on the Social Road, you can have a powerful and prestigious Tier 1 elite job managing big government, or you can have a public employee union or bureaucratic Tier 2 job keeping big government running, or you can sit back and have a Tier 3 welfare "job" and let big government provide you with transfer payments to pay your bills. Or, you can choose to tough it out in a private sector job and help fund the welfare state with your hard work and high taxes.

That's work on the Social Road. Where do you fit in today? In the future, where do you want to fit in? Tier 1? Tier 2? Tier 3? Or, do you want to languish in the private sector under progressive socialism? Of course, you can choose the Free Way discussed in Chapter 2 instead.

Let's next turn our attention to the topic of the Social Road and your money.

The Social Road and Your Money

There's no doubt that the Social Road has a profound impact on your money and your checkbook. First, we can start with taxes. You can always expect very high taxes on the Social Road. That's a given. Progressives want and need high taxes to pay for their economic vision of the Good Life. It's obviously true. Big government requires big bucks. There's no way around it. We can enumerate a long list of taxes we currently pay to finance big government and its progressive welfare state programs. Expect the list to get longer on the Social Road.

Income taxes, Social Security taxes, Medicare taxes, corporate taxes, investment taxes as well as a myriad of other taxes including: sales taxes, phones taxes, cable TV taxes, property taxes on your home or your home-based business, car registration taxes, gasoline taxes, natural gas taxes, electricity taxes, water taxes, sewer taxes, and even death (or estate) taxes – assuming you have any money left when you die and when you finish paying all the other taxes demanded by big government. All these taxes and countless other taxes pull dollars from the private sector (aka, your checkbook) into big government's coffers. Also, big government frequently wants to raise your taxes, as if you don't pay enough taxes already.

In addition, it seems like new taxes are constantly being considered or added. These currently include taxes on services such as car repairs, health club memberships, tickets to movies, golf courses, tax preparation, accounting services, consulting services, and legal services. This is not to mention a whole host of potentially new and economically devastating environmental taxes, like carbon taxes and cap-and-trade taxes that today's progressives are eager to impose on you and your family – destroying your lifestyle and potentially turning America into a third world country.

Plus, who can ignore the newly created taxes on tanning, health plans, health insurance companies, drug companies, and medical device manufacturers, all found in the 2010 health care law that creates a *de facto* government-controlled, health care rationing system that raises taxes, raises costs, and impedes innovation. We won't even attempt here to put a price tag on the health care law's impact on big government deficits and debt levels. But, you can bet that the impact will be substantial.

By the way, you might not have thought of it this way before, but inflation is an insidious and hidden tax brought to you by big government. By following a monetary policy that increases the money supply above certain reasonable limits, or by *talking down* the dollar, big government can create inflation. The subsequent decline in the buying power of your money is the economic equivalent of taxing away part of your wealth (whether you are middle income, rich, or poor).

While inflation is currently not an issue in the news, in the near future, one big government policy option for dealing with the mounting and spiraling high, deficit-spending and the outrageous big government debt levels is to *monetize* the problem with inflation. What does it mean to "monetize" the problem? Essentially, the deficits and debt are brought down by making the dollar worth less. This, in turn, makes the deficits and debt worth less. How does this work?

From an economic point of view, if we owe $1 Trillion (we should be so fortunate to owe so little) and if the dollar's value is brought down through inflation, then big government can pay down the $1 Trillion debt with "less valuable" dollars. It's all smoke and mirrors at the big government level. But, for citizens, inflation is bad news. We all have to pay more for groceries and gasoline and clothing and all our other needs because the dollars in our checking account are less valuable. Moreover, if you have savings, investments, a 401(k), or an IRA, the value of your nest egg is also lower. Inflation robs savers and investors of the value of their savings and investments.

Bottom line, inflation is just another big government tax on all of us and another economic pothole on the Social Road.

Besides numerous high taxes and the special, hidden tax of inflation, there is another speed bump on the Social Road known as deflation. Its risks are not as well known as are the risks associated with inflation. But, its effects can be quite traumatic to a family's budget. Deflation is simply the reduction in general price levels or sometimes in asset price levels. The causes of deflation can be a decrease in the monetary supply below an unhealthy level as was the case with the Great Depression. This is done by big government through its monetary policy. Or, deflation can be caused by other factors such as fear over our economic future. If America goes down the Social Road, you might feel deflation if the value of your home decreases or if your pay is cut.

Today, we find that big government is creating a great deal of fear, uncertainty and doubt about our economic future in the minds of citizens. Reasons for these fears include big government stimulus spending that appears reckless; deficits that seem to be unbearable; and big government debt levels that look economically unsustainable. Moreover, programs such as Medicare have incredibly high unfunded liabilities. Medicare's unfunded liability was recently pegged at about $38 Trillion and growing at a rate of 21% per year! Do you think Medicare will go bankrupt? What kind of economic burden is being given to our children and grand children?

In addition, many States and cities in the U. S. are facing significant budgetary crises and some are teetering on the brink of bankruptcy. In many cases, States and cities might not even be able to afford to pay for their own basic and vital services, let alone huge public employee union pension benefits.

Moreover, with the *de facto* socialization of our health care system and the over-regulation of many aspects of our economy and lives, citizens are holding back on spending, fearful of the future. This subsequent reduction in spending amounts to a downward demand for products and services, and ultimately, a decline in prices for certain assets. Of course, this has a depressing effect on the overall economy. When consumers stop spending, prices fall, businesses lose sales, employees lose jobs, and consumers default on mortgages and loans.

It's really quite a combination. Because of big government fiscal policies (spending and taxing policies) as well as monetary policies (money supply and interest rate policies), we might face both asset deflation and inflation problems in the near future. Is it any wonder why so many citizens experience fear, uncertainty, and doubt? Is it any wonder why the Social Road always leads to economic bankruptcy?

In fact, the Social Road is a rough road for your money and your economic security. High taxes eat away your earnings, leaving you with less take home pay. Big government fiscal and monetary policies can also wreck your retirement plans and devastate your saving, investment, and retirement funds. Plus, these policies can decimate the overall economy and burden your children and grand children with a legacy of high debt. Needless to say, expect your standard of living and lifestyle to decline on the Social Road as well.

The Social Road and Your Lifestyle

Your lifestyle will change dramatically as you travel down the Social Road. As your freedoms erode, as your job opportunities and income diminish, as your money goes to pay higher and higher taxes, and as your economic security fades, your standard of living and your lifestyle will decline precipitously. It's the inevitable price of traveling on the Social Road.

Progressive socialists will feel a sense of achievement when everyone lives in shared poverty. Their vision of equal outcomes for all people – regardless of substantive differences in individuals' skills and abilities, education and training, knowledge and intelligence, motivation and effort, and just plain old hard work – will become a reality they have sought for over a century. Of course, progressive socialist elites will always take care of their own personal needs. Their lifestyle will be enhanced, not diminished as yours will be.

All the factors discussed in previous sections in this book will play a part in cutting down your standard of living and lifestyle. But, quite possibly, the most important factor will be the nationalization of the American energy industry, if it happens. If big government takes over the energy sector of our economy, big government will control virtually all activity. Why?

It's simple and it's intuitive. Energy runs our economy. Energy powers our lives.

It's true. Energy powers our homes. Energy feeds our families – agriculture, food production, beverages, and restaurants. Energy fuels our transportation – cars, trucks, SUVs, trains, subways, and jets. Energy builds our structures – homes, farms, office buildings, factories, and recreational facilities. Energy makes us look and feel better – clothing, shoes, personal care, cosmetics, and beauty products. Energy connects us – phones, cell phones, smart phones, telecommunications infrastructure, and the internet.

Energy runs our industries – computers, high tech, aerospace, defense, autos, trucks, boats, construction equipment, mining, metals, manufacturing, paints, wood products, and tools. Energy informs and entertains us – books, newspapers, magazines, TV, radio, satellite, internet, toys, games, hobbies, sports, travel, and other recreational activities. Energy diagnoses and heals us – hospitals, medical technology, dental technology, contact lenses, eye wear, and pharmaceuticals.

Energy even empowers our energy industry itself – oil and gas, exploration, drilling, refining, transportation, electric power distribution, coal, nuclear, solar, wind, and biofuels.

As this book is being written, various cap-and-trade proposals and carbon tax programs have been suggested and debated. At the core of these programs is the attempt by environmental socialists and progressive socialists to nationalize (or socialize, if you prefer) the American energy industry. Without question, such programs will ration energy usage all across America. Big government will control how much energy and what kinds of energy each and every person and business will be allowed to use by out-of-touch, big government bureaucrats. The opportunity for favoritism, cronyism, bribery, and corruption will be rampant as well.

Will your personal energy cap permit you to own an SUV? Will you be able to run your air conditioner for more than one hour during a hot summer's day? Will you be able to drive to the mountains for a summer vacation? Or, fly to Florida or Hawaii or any other warm spot for a winter vacation?

Will you face gasoline prices that exceed $7 a gallon next year? Will a 25% carbon tax be placed on your natural gas usage? Will you be able to afford to heat your home? Will your home mortgage interest deduction be phased out gradually based on the square footage of your home (to encourage you to lessen your "carbon footprint")? Will the equity in your home decline dramatically?

Whether a business can get access to carbon or energy rations will determine if it can go into business in the first place or continue to stay in business if it already exists. Which businesses will big government favor? Which businesses will it permit? Which businesses will be put out of business by big government? Which businesses will be taken over by big government?

If big government controls the energy industry, it will control the heart of America – the life blood of American individuality, free enterprise, and freedom. It will control your standard of living, your lifestyle, and it will limit your ability to enjoy life and to be free. The profound words in The Declaration of Independence:

"WE hold these Truths to be self-evident, that all Men are created equal, that they are endowed by their Creator with certain unalienable Rights, that among these are Life, Liberty, and the Pursuit of Happiness"

will have been ignored and essentially removed from American life. You will no longer be able to pursue happiness as you choose. Your unalienable rights will have been diminished beyond recognition and relevance.

Your lifestyle on the Social Road is likely to look a lot more like life under a totalitarian regime, and certainly nothing like the America our Founding Fathers envisioned in The Declaration of Independence and the Constitution.

Finally, let's look at health on the Social Road.

The Social Road and Your Health

Don't expect great health care on the Social Road. It's not going to happen. Don't expect the same patient-doctor relationship you've experienced in the past. That will disappear quickly. You might never see the same doctor twice in a row, or twice in your entire lifetime. It's even possible you will rarely see a doctor at all. On the Social Road, you might be limited to seeing a physician's assistant or a nurse, or just talking to a health care provider on the phone.

In fact, if the 2010 health care law is not repealed or ruled unconstitutional (and it is clearly unconstitutional), big government will control and ration health care for all Americans, except for the elites running big government who will be given superior health care. Tier 1 elites always receive better treatment. That's progressive socialism.

Make no mistake about it, despite platitudes and hand-waving, the 2010 health care law is the de facto nationalization (or socialization) of the American health care industry. It will likely take years to fully implement. But, it is socialized medicine. It is progressive socialism. It is a system of health care rationing.

You and some of your family member's lives might be cut short by this system of health care rationing that will guarantee shortages and inferior health care. Whether you live or die someday might be a decision effectively made by a cold-hearted bureaucrat in Washington.

This law will take away your health care freedom and that means your choices will be severely restricted. You will have few, if any, options. Indeed, your choices will be strictly limited – your choice of doctors, your choice of hospitals, your choice of treatments, your choice of tests, your choice of drugs, your choice of health insurance plans, and your choice of health insurance coverage.

Doctors will be given significantly fewer options too. They will be restricted in their testing and treatment decisions and in a myriad of other ways.

Plus, the entire patient-doctor business model will be radically overturned. Instead of an individual doctor working for an individual patient, all doctors will be working for big government. Notice how the patient is no longer in control. The patient can't fire a doctor with bad bedside manner, and the patient can't fire the big government bureaucrats that set the rules and regulations that the patient must dutifully follow. The patient is powerless and helpless against the big government, and the doctors who are directly or indirectly Tier 2 employees of the big government. So much, for patient-focused health care. That's progressive socialism.

There is enormous data available on how socialized health care works in Britain and Canada. Actually, it is more accurate to say how socialized health care DOESN'T work in Britain and Canada. Stories of inadequate health care are legion. For example, tens of thousands of British citizens potentially going blind because they were being denied a certain drug for their eye disease. Or, people being denied drugs that might increase their chances of surviving cancer. Let's look at one story that remarkably illustrates the cruelty of socialized medicine.

According to the Heritage Foundation, Linda, a patient with bowel cancer, was told by her doctors that a certain drug called cetuximab might help her to live. But, Britain's National Institute of Health and Clinical Excellence (NICE) – the group in charge of rationing health care – did not consider the drug cost-effective and would not approve its use. Hoping to live, Linda used her own savings to purchase the drug anyway. When big government bureaucrats found out what Linda had done, they denied her treatment and she died within a few months. How utterly cruel, inhumane, and heartless. How bitterly ironic to call the agency in charge of limiting health care and causing untold deaths, NICE. That's how progressives distort language and that's what health is like when you go down the Social Road. That's progressive socialism.

In reality, that's one woman's life story and you might think it's purely anecdotal. But, the harsh reality is that cancer survival rates are significantly lower in Britain. On the Social Road, we can expect our cancer survival rates to decline as well.

Expect less innovation in health care testing, treatments, medical devices, and pharmaceuticals on the Social Road. Why? Because without the incentives of the free market and the capital for investment in private sector businesses, there will be much less ability and motivation to innovate. Future potential health care improvements will be impeded and curtailed.

Not only will the quantity and quality of our health care be hurt badly on the Social Road, but costs will go through the roof. We can look toward Britain, Canada, and the Massachusetts universal health care plan as proof points for skyrocketing costs, or we can look at it from an economic point of view.

Costs will increase under socialized medicine for two reasons: (1) supplies of health care products and services are lower, and (2) demand for health care products and services are higher. Basic economics. Simple stuff really. Supplies are lower because free market incentives to increase supplies are eliminated. Demand is higher because everyone is forced to participate in the program.

Does anyone really think that big government can run the American health care industry better than free enterprise? The American health care industry is nearly 20% of the American economy. Remember, too, this is the same big government that now runs Medicare with its $38 Trillion unfunded liability, growing at an alarming rate of 21% per year.

Certainly, most progressive socialists know that big government can't run the entire American health care industry as well as the private sector. But, they still persist in their flawed economic vision – a vision of a "socialist utopia." In health care, this economic vision leads to shortages and rationing. Overall, it results in shared poverty for all, but the few elites at the top of big government.

Indeed, on the Social Road, you can expect your health care to be limited and rationed. You can expect your quality of health care to be substantially lower, and you can expect your costs to be substantially higher. Also, you can expect your patient-doctor relationship to be history. This is the health care price Americans will pay, if America chooses to go down the Social Road.

Let's summarize the Social Road and the claim it's a path to the Good

Life.

The Social Road to Moral and Economic Bankruptcy

While progressive socialists paint the Social Road with good intentions and uplifting, moral language, it nonetheless leads to moral and economic bankruptcy. Progressives need to use a steady stream of deceit, deception and fear to drag people down the dark alley of socialism. Progressives do this to mislead citizens into thinking the Social Road will be scenic and beautiful, with lavish economic benefits for all, without the inconvenience of ever taking an entrepreneurial risk, or working hard at a regular, day-to-day job.

In reality, progressives must hide socialism's inherently flawed philosophical system that often results in favoritism, cronyism, bribery, and corruption. Importantly, it must always cover up the economic facts of life. As an economic system, socialism is a failure – both theoretically and in practice. Socialism fails everywhere it's tried. It might take some time to fail in certain places. But, progressive socialism always leads to moral and economic bankruptcy.

What does the Social Road mean in practical terms to you? What does it mean – in terms of freedom, jobs, money, lifestyle, and health – to you?

The Social Road means big government and limited freedoms – religious freedom, political freedom, economic freedom, and intellectual freedom. The Social Road means fewer jobs in the private sector. It means much higher taxes. It means the real possibility of asset deflation in the short run – your home might drop in value and your pay might be cut as well. It also means the potential for high inflation in the long run – your costs for everything else might increase. The Social Road means very high big government spending, very high big government deficits, very high big government debt, and much lower economic growth for everyone. It means a lower standard of living and a precipitous decline in your lifestyle. It means health care rationing for you and your family. It also means lower health care quality at higher costs.

Clearly, the Social Road does not lead to the Good Life.

Fortunately, there is a better alternative for all of us, the Free Way. Let's turn our attention now to the Free Way.

Chapter 2

The Free Way

"Now the Lord is the Spirit, and where the Spirit of the Lord is,
there is freedom."
2 Corinthians 3:17

The Free Way leads to economic growth and prosperity. It also leads to peace and harmony among nations. It is the path to the Good Life.

The Free Way is all about freedom – religious freedom, political freedom, economic freedom, and intellectual freedom – and how these freedoms are inextricably linked together to help create economic growth, prosperity, and peace.

While it goes beyond the scope of this book, freedom is a gift from God and the freedom that America enjoys from its founding can be historically traced to America's Christian and Jewish heritage. For readers who would like to better understand our heritage of freedom, please consider reading my book: *America's Economic War – Your Freedom, Money and Life.*

What is the Free Way to the Good Life? Why is this economic vision so much better than the Social Road? Why does it lead to economic growth, prosperity, and peace? Let's answer these questions by looking at how the Free Way impacts five important areas of our lives: freedom, jobs, money, lifestyle, and health.

The Free Way – Your Freedom and Limited Government

In stark contrast to the proponents of the Social Road, advocates for the Free Way believe that the Good Life is best achieved through freedom and limited government. They deeply believe in both the goodness and the wisdom of individuals. They trust people.

The advocates for the Free Way think individuals are smart, not stupid.

They think individuals should make their own decisions, not big government bureaucrats. They think individuals should plan their own lives freely, without big government looking over their shoulders. They think individuals should take their own risks freely as they deem appropriate, without big government interference. They certainly don't believe big government needs to regulate every aspect and every detail of every person's life. They also don't believe big government must protect every citizen from every potential hazard and risk in life.

Advocates for the Free Way believe individual citizens are responsible, trustworthy, intelligent, and can manage their own lives without insidious, big government intrusion and intervention.

The advocates for the Free Way go by many different names – conservatives, economic conservatives, social conservatives, neo-conservatives, libertarians, classic liberals, Constitutional originalists, even capitalists – to name a few. The simple label conservative is probably the most popular term in use today for describing advocates for the Free Way.

> > > Not All "Conservatives" are Conservative

Lots of people who call themselves "conservative" are truly not conservative. Often, their economic vision is more aligned with the Social Road. Generally, these people want to go down the Social Road more slowly or in a more measured way than their progressive quasi-allies. These are not advocates for the Free Way. Their support for the Social Road is more tepid and only relatively more conservative than progressives. They are definitely not true advocates for the Free Way.

Sometimes too, progressives use the term "conservative" to falsely describe themselves, because the term conservative resonates with most Americans and because it makes these progressives appear to support our nation's founding principles. However, when progressives call themselves "conservative" or use "conservative" language, it is because they are uncomfortable being honest with you and me. They know Americans are strong believers in freedom. They know American's will quickly reject their progressive ideas, plans, and programs, if Americans are aware that their individual freedoms will be limited or eliminated altogether.

Choosing the Good Life

To illustrate this point, consider the recently enacted 2010 health care law. Americans in poll after poll rejected this bill before it became law. Despite their opposition and over their objections to socialized medicine, it was passed by both the House and Senate and signed into law by the president.

American citizens are smart. They recognize the fact that this progressive plan to ration health care will limit their health care freedom. It remains to be seen if this law will be ruled unconstitutional or will be repealed by a future Congress. But, it is unlikely to stand because the American people were against it from the outset.

>>> Not All Conservatives Seek the Same Size of Government

Of course, not all advocates of the Free Way seek the precise same degree of freedom and the exact same size of government. Mileage may vary, as they say. But, they do share a common vision for individual freedom and smaller, more limited government.

Advocates for the Free Way believe in limited government that performs certain basic functions and performs these functions well. These include protecting the nation from external threats (such as war and terrorism) and protecting the nation from internal threats (such as violence and crime). In addition and very importantly, advocates for the Free Way strongly believe the role of government is to preserve, protect, and defend the Constitution and all of our freedoms, and to do so, under the Rule of Law.

>>> Conservatives Believe in Freedom of Speech

Advocates for the Free Way believe in the Constitutionally-protected Freedom of Speech, including the freedom to say things that might offend someone else. Politically correct speech, "hate speech," the "Fairness Doctrine," Net Neutrality (aka "Web Fairness Doctrine"), campaign finance reform, and stifling academic freedom on campuses, – all are attempts by proponents of the Social Road to limit or eliminate Freedom of Speech. Advocates for the Free Way seek Freedom of Speech over speech limitations.

Limiting someone's Freedom of Speech is a clear violation of the First Amendment. If a priest, for example, believes in accordance with Catholic teachings that abortion is immoral, why shouldn't the priest have the freedom to express that view in the pulpit, or in public? In a similar way, if a minister in a Baptist church wants to preach on homosexuality, why shouldn't that minister have the freedom to do so? Yes, some people will disagree with the priest's views or the minister's interpretation of Scripture. To some homosexuals, the latter might be offensive or "hateful" from their vantage point. But, to claim any speech, whether in church or in the Public Square, is "hate speech" and therefore, must be silenced, is Constitutionally wrong and a violation of the individual's Freedom of Speech.

After all, hate is a moral wrong. As long as it does not cross the line into, for example, bodily harm to another individual, it should not be a legal matter. It's a spiritual matter within a person's soul. It's a spiritual matter for God. It's not a legal matter for big government to judge or control. Big government should not be in the business of trying to prevent hurt feelings. However, advocates for the Free Way do think it is the province of limited government to protect individuals from physical injury or harm.

Indeed, chances are any statement of any opinion, will offend someone, somewhere, at some time. How preposterous to pick a few topics and call those statements "hate speech." Plus, who is to determine what speech is "hate speech?" Big government? Progressive elites?

Besides, advocates for the Free Way believe that people are bound to disagree on a multitude of issues. Strong opinions on controversial topics don't necessarily mean hate is involved. People are different. They have different opinions, feelings, and thoughts. They should be free to express their thoughts and feelings, however controversial or politically incorrect. Plus, even if there is hate in someone's heart, they should still have Freedom of Speech. Others can probably recognize that hate rather easily and treat the opinion appropriately.

Conservatives on the Free Way adamantly support Free Speech and staunchly oppose big government regulation of speech. But, why are progressives on the Social Road so afraid of free speech anyway? Why are they so afraid of ideas and opinions? Progressive intellectuals, of all people, especially those working in universities and colleges, should be the most open to ideas and opinions and learning. Why are they so afraid of academic freedom for all professors and students? Same thing in K-12 education – why are some teachers so afraid of ideas that are not politically correct (aka progressively correct)?

As an example, why was a student in a public policy class threatened with getting an "F" for the class if she attended a conservative political conference? So much for real education where professors lead open-minded discussions, and classes freely debate the issues of the day.

On the Free Way, both professors and students have intellectual freedom and enjoy the discovery of old and new, ideas and insights. Opinions are shared. Light bulbs turn on. Knowledge is gained. Learning is enhanced. Growth occurs in an enlightened atmosphere. On the Free Way, we have education in our schools, colleges, and universities. Unfortunately, on the Social Road, education morphs into progressive indoctrination and training.

Why are progressives on the Social Road so afraid of free speech? Is it because free speech will reveal some truth? Or, are progressives fearful everyone won't agree with them? Are they fearful that they will lose control of the economic agenda? The political agenda? The religious/cultural agenda? Are they afraid they won't control big government and all of our lives?

>>> Conservatives Believe in Religious Freedom

On the Free Way, it's true, conservatives believe in Freedom of Speech. It's also true that they believe in Freedom of Religion and the Freedom of Religious Expression. On the Social Road in sharp contrast, progressives believe in Freedom FROM Religion where any semblance of religious expression is methodically banned from the Public Square and public debate. Some progressives even speak about "freedom of worship" as if to imply that Freedom of Religion and Freedom of Religious Expression must be limited only to a church, synagogue, temple, or mosque. By so doing, progressives actively deny and attempt to limit our religious freedom that is so vital to both our culture and civilization.

On the Social Road, a nation that limits citizens to "freedom of worship" rather than Freedom of Religion and Freedom of Religious Expression might not permit a young girl from a wearing a Cross necklace to school. Or, it might not allow you to bury a relative in a grave marked with a Cross. Or, it might not sanction a whole host of other religious expressions in public, such as public prayer.

This is a direct, frontal assault on the original intent and meaning of the Constitution's First Amendment. It can't be tolerated in a free society and it is a clear violation and misinterpretation of the Constitution. Advocates for the Free Way want Freedom of Religion and Freedom of Religious Expression to flourish in America. Of course, this is not State-sponsored religion. It's simply religious freedom.

>>> Conservatives Believe in Economic Freedom

Advocates of the Free Way also believe in economic freedom for every citizen and they believe in the sanctity of every person's private property – one of the key requirements for economic freedom.

Early socialists such as Karl Marx and Frederick Engels thought private property should be abolished. But, if big government owns all property as they wanted, there can be no private property, only public property. Without private property, individuals can't buy, sell, own, keep, use, and donate private property. Without private property, there can be no free enterprise, no free markets, and no free trade – in short, there can be no economic freedom, because there is no property that can be the object of economic transactions in a free market.

An important point to remember is that high taxes are a form of big government confiscation of private property. If your total tax bill is high, big government is taking away your private property every year. Money in your checking account (or money you never see in your checking account, due to tax withholding) represents purchasing power. It is the equivalent of private property you will never be able to acquire and subsequently use.

If you're curious to see how high your taxes really are today, just get out all your records and receipts and try to calculate your total tax bill for a month or a year. Be sure to include payroll taxes, property taxes, sales taxes, cable TV taxes, phone taxes, car registration taxes, gasoline taxes, and the myriad of other taxes you most likely pay big government. You probably will be surprised – if not shocked – by the percent of your income that goes out to big government. Plus, as we are ready to go into 2011, taxes are poised to go much higher than in 2010.

In contrast to progressives, advocates for the Free Way believe in private property, free enterprise, free markets, and free trade. They believe in economic freedom. They believe citizens should be free to buy, sell, own, keep, use, and donate private property at their own discretion. They also believe that there are some circumstances under which limited government can be involved in the free market to assure the public's safety and to avoid fraud. But, these circumstances need to be strictly limited to avoid any major loss of economic freedom.

Conservatives view many environmental and energy regulations as an undue burden on individuals and on the American economy, limiting economic activity and economic freedom. For example, cutting off critical irrigation water to farmers with restrictive and unrealistic, big government regulations, reduces farmers' incomes and reduces the private property values of their farms. If that's not enough, it also reduces the supplies of food to grocery stores and it raises the price of food you purchase for your family.

Conservatives also see excessive environmental and energy regulations as a method to limit your right to use your own private property. A fundamental part of owning private property is the freedom to use it. After all, what good is owning a farm, if big government cuts off your irrigation water? You can't raise crops and you can't make a living. Your private property, in effect, is controlled by big government. Big government *owns* your property, when it *controls* your property.

Plus, the administrative costs of regulations can be staggering as well. Examples abound of damage done to the economy through big government environmental and energy regulations. One estimate places the cost of all big government regulations on the American economy as exceeding $1 Trillion annually. From an economic point of view, consider the cost of big government regulations as another tax on the American economy that we all pay eventually.

On the Free Way, the needs of individuals and the economy are balanced against the needs of the environment. Free market incentives are always available to develop new environmental and energy technologies to protect our natural resources, while meeting the day-to-day needs of consumers and businesses. Limited government provides reasonable incentives to encourage those goals as well.

Unless we choose to go backwards in time to life centuries ago, or we choose to live a more primitive lifestyle, we need to make reasonable economic tradeoffs among the competing choices that progress, innovation, and technology offer us.

How many people would choose to stop making pain-killing anesthetics and life-saving drugs for the sake of the environment? Don't most people think these products are worth the costs? In another example, how many people are willing to give up driving cars, using subways, and flying jets to help lessen any impacts these modes of transportation have on the environment? Not many I think. By the way, how many big government elites are willing to give up their luxury lifestyles for the environment? If not, why should any of us give up our lifestyles either?

Economics comes down to making choices every day. In fact, life is all about economic choices. The Free Way believes the best people to make economic choices are individuals, acting freely. The Social Road doesn't believe you will make the best decisions. The Social Road believes in big government. Of course, we all know how efficient big government is when it comes to managing anything.

In another area, conservatives believe that eminent domain – the taking of private property by the government – must be constitutionally limited. The Fifth Amendment clearly explains what is constitutional taking of private property:

No person shall ... be deprived of life, liberty, or property, without due process of law; nor shall private property be taken for public use, without just compensation.

Unfortunately, today, the Fifth Amendment has been gutted by progressive court decisions such as *Kelo v. City of New London*. This Supreme Court ruling has made it possible now for big government to take nearly any private property from a citizen and use it to benefit another private party in the interests of so-called economic development (aka, tax revenues to big government). So much for private property.

> > > Conservatives Believe in Other Freedoms

Advocates for the Free Way believe in a whole host of other freedoms including the Freedom to Keep and Bear Arms, protected by the Second Amendment.

Conservatives seek to keep and, in some cases, to restore America to the Free Way in which our freedoms – religious freedom, political freedom, economic freedom, and intellectual freedom – are all guaranteed by the Constitution and are all upheld under the Rule of Law.

Bottom line, the economic vision on the Free Way is for all Americans to have Constitutionally-guaranteed and protected freedom, to live under the Rule of Law, and to have limited government. You and your family can take a deep breath and breathe the air of freedom on the Free Way. Not so, on the Social Road to totalitarianism and bankruptcy.

That's a brief synopsis of the Free Way and its impact in the areas of freedom and limited government.

Let's now turn our attention to another important area of our lives – jobs.

The Free Way and Your Job

On the Free Way, the sky is the limit when it comes to jobs. More jobs. Better jobs. Higher paying jobs. More opportunities. Better opportunities. Lots of choices. Lots of chances to build your own economic security and your own economic wealth, if that's your goal. The market offers countless opportunities, you decide which ones to pursue.

On the Free Way, your opportunities are virtually limitless. In fact, they are probably limited most by your own ambition, motivation, skills, intelligence, education, and desire to work hard. You set your own limits. You set your own goals. A big government doesn't throttle back your dreams with endless rules, regulations, and red tape.

On the Free Way, you have economic freedom. You have the chance to decide where you will best fit into the market today, and next year, and in five years.

On the Free Way, you also have lower taxes on economic growth – specifically taxes on income, savings, and investment. That's part of the economic vision of the Free Way. Lower taxes have a substantial positive impact on new job creation. As mentioned earlier, the Harding-Coolidge tax cuts, the post World War II tax cuts, the JFK tax cuts, the Reagan tax cuts, and the Bush tax cuts, spurred economic growth and new job creation.

To illustrate the relationship between tax cuts and jobs, consider the Reagan tax cuts. Let's look at the years 1982 – 2007. Arthur B. Laffer, Stephen Moore, and Peter J. Tanous call these years the "Twenty-Five-Year Boom" in their book, *The End of Prosperity: How Higher Taxes Will Doom the Economy – If We Let It Happen*. During this period, they indicate that U. S. wealth grew from $25 Trillion to nearly $57 Trillion. Indeed, it was the greatest period of wealth creation in the history of the world. It followed Ronald Reagan's wise tax cuts and other supporting fiscal and monetary policies, sometimes called *Reaganomics*. Incidentally, during the Reagan years, 1981 – 1989, 17 million new jobs were created according to the authors.

Today's high unemployment rate around 9.5% (as I'm writing this book) goes hand-in-hand with today's high (and apparently still growing) tax burden on the American people. Once again, expect more jobs and better jobs on the Free Way.

What kind of jobs does the Free Way offer you? For starters, you can work for someone else – typically, a small business, a medium-sized business, or a large global corporation. You get a steady paycheck, usually some benefits, maybe a lot of benefits. In a free market, businesses are competing for your labor services. So, you can shop around for the best job and change jobs if and when you like.

Note that I'm writing now about jobs on the Free Way, where jobs are plentiful and abundant because the market is free to create new jobs. You wouldn't have nearly as many choices under a high tax, job-killing, progressive socialist, big government.

The second type of job on the Free Way is that of an entrepreneur. You might choose to be self-employed and create your own small business with just one employee – you. If you're self-employed, your income might vary from month-to-month. But, you have enormous freedom to do what you enjoy. Plus, you have an unlimited upside potential. If your product or service is a hit with consumers or businesses, you might be retiring soon to a tropical island.

Your idea of entrepreneurship might not be a one-person business. It might be to start a new corporation. You might need to get help from family and friends, angel investors, and/or venture capitalists. You might be attending college and get an idea for a new business. You might, for example, be like two Stanford graduate students, Larry Page and Sergey Brin, who had maxed-out their credit cards and sought out Andy Bechtolsheim for help. Andy's $100,000 check helped launch Google. At the time of writing this book, Google's market cap is approximately $156 Billion – not bad considering they started out with maxed-out credit cards.

Third, you might enjoy being an investor. On the Free Way, your full-time (or part-time) occupation might be to take your savings and invest in promising businesses or corporations. You might prefer the security of certain bonds. Or, the risk-reward profile of other types of investments. You can start small with a few dollars and work your way toward a significant-sized portfolio. Someone once asked a well known and successful "student" of the stock market how much time was needed to become a successful investor. His quick answer – How much do you want to succeed?

On the Free Way, a fourth job is to become a venture capitalist. Venture capitalists are a special type of investor that often brings together money from other investors, and often provides direct management assistance to start-up companies. Venture capitalists play an important role in the free market – capital formation – bringing together capital from different sources for the purpose of investing in new businesses. It takes capital to launch new businesses. Venture capitalists are one vital means toward capital formation and the creation of new businesses (and new jobs too). Of course, VCs (as they are called) can be wildly successful themselves, if they invest in the right start-ups.

So, on the Free Way, whether you choose to be an employee of a business or corporation, whether you choose to be a self-employed entrepreneur or a start-up corporate entrepreneur, whether you choose to be an investor, or whether you choose to be a venture capitalist, it's your choice. Employee. Entrepreneur. Investor. Venture Capitalist. On the

Free Way, they are all avenues to the Good Life.

It's also worth repeating that on the Free Way, everyone who wants a job can have a job. That might be difficult for some people to believe. But, it's true. In any economy, there are always things that need to be done. There are always jobs to do. If there are no big government rules, regulations, and restrictions to filling those jobs, the economy will absorb all the people who want to work. Employees might not get the exact pay they want, the exact job they desire, or the exact location they prefer, but they will get a job.

For example, maybe an inner city teenager would like to work at a small shoe store during the summer. Maybe, the owner of that shoe store can only afford to pay $5.00 per hour. If big government forces the store owner to pay $7.25 to any employee (plus taxes), the store will have to forego hiring the teenager and the teenager will be unemployed. This is a lose-lose situation.

In fact, minimum wage laws help to cause unemployment because they keep less skilled people from obtaining entry-level employment. They also hurt small businesses that can only afford smaller payrolls, from getting the help they need to grow into bigger businesses with larger payrolls. If the teenager and shoe store owner would both benefit from a $5.00 per hour hourly rate AND they both freely agree to such an arrangement, why should big government get in their way? It certainly doesn't help the teenager, the shoe store owner, or the economy.

As the simple example above illustrates, burdensome big government regulations prevent jobs from being created. Also, big government high taxes prevent jobs from being created by pulling money out of the private sector and giving it to economically inefficient and ineffective, big government programs. Fortunately, on the Free Way, there are always jobs for those who want to work. On the Social Road, expect chronic, high unemployment instead.

Finally, of course, the Free Way offers significant economic incentives for new business creation and new job creation. Profits motivate many people to improve their life and their family's lives through hard work and innovation, while at the same time providing their neighbors with needed products and services. That's another reason why there are more jobs on the Free Way.

For all these reasons and many more, the Free Way is the best economic vision for job creation. It's also one reason why the Free Way leads to economic growth and prosperity as well as the peace that springs forth from economic abundance.

How does the Free Way impact your money? Let's look at the Free Way and your money next.

The Free Way and Your Money

On the Free Way, the economy soars. With economic freedom and limited government, we have substantial and real economic growth. Taxes on economic growth – namely, taxes on income, savings, and investment – are all substantially lower than on the Social Road. With more money available in the private sector, we get more capital available for investment in new businesses, new jobs, and new economic growth. With more money in your checking account, you have more money to spend and you also help create economic growth for the economy with every purchase you make.

The result is simple. On the Free Way, we get widespread and general prosperity. We see more peace among individuals within a nation, and we see more peace among nations that travel together on the Free Way. Have you ever seen a free nation militarily attack another free nation, where both nations participate in free trade? It doesn't happen because freedom and prosperity generally breed peace, not war.

Of course, for individuals, life on the Free Way is better, more prosperous, and more economically secure. People are generally more optimistic for their economic futures too. Expect to have more opportunities, more money, more wealth, and more security on the Free Way. Expect a higher standard of living and a constantly-improving lifestyle.

For those dealing with special life issues and for those who need a helping hand, charitable giving is higher on the Free Way as well. On the Free Way, individuals are more compassionate and more generous. In fact, America has traditionally been the most generous nation the world has ever known. When there is a natural disaster anywhere in the world, America rushes to the rescue.

In addition, limited government tax revenues are typically higher on the Free Way than on the Social Road, because economic growth is higher and because lower marginal tax rates on income, savings, and investment encourage economic growth. Surprisingly, with lower tax rates, often come higher tax revenues.

So, with more charitable giving to private groups and with higher tax revenues, people who need help receive more benefits on the Free Way. Plus, the needs are met with less bureaucratic paperwork and fewer strings attached. Moreover, people who require help are treated with more human dignity and greater respect on the Free Way.

Two other reasons why charitable giving is higher on the Free Way – one might be obvious, one might surprise you. First, the obvious reason. When people have more money, they have more money to give away to good causes. Second, the surprising reason. On the Social Road, people learn to become victims and people learn to expect big government to supply everyone's needs. Relative to the Free Way, potential donors are less inclined to feel an obligation to help others. People are more generous on the Free Way.

The economic vision for the Free Way is bullish. It's positive, upbeat, and optimistic. It also works in the real world. It's not utopian or dysfunctional as it is on the Social Road. Importantly, the Free Way doesn't require deceit, deception, and fear to convince people its progressive ideas are valuable. The Free Way stands on sound economic theory and on solid economic data.

On the Free Way, expect to have a better economy, a brighter future, and more money in your checking account.

How does the economic vision for the Free Way impact your lifestyle. That's our next topic.

The Free Way and Your Lifestyle

On the Free Way, with economic growth and prosperity, come both a better lifestyle and a higher standard of living. Indeed, living with economic freedom means your life will be filled with more opportunities to choose what you want to do with your life, as well as the means to pursue the choices you make. For many that will mean not just finding happiness in their own personal activities and achievements, but serving others through charitable and philanthropic work in America and around the world.

Living in an America with limited government that focuses on pro-growth policies means living with a strong economy, steady growth, and solid economic security. Knowing you have a stable job, low inflation, increasing home equity, reliable investments, and a retirement plan that is certain, all contribute to your economic peace of mind and security.

On the Free Way, expect the quality and quantity of consumer goods and services you purchase to increase every year, relative to the number of hours you need to work to pay for them. Your purchasing power continually improves on the Free Way. This is due in some measure to increasing productivity that results from higher capital investment in business. When capital is invested in a business, labor productivity and pay typically jump up.

On the Free Way, expect more leisure activity (if you want more leisure time) and more options to use that free time. Expect entertainment and recreational activities to abound and expect to pay relatively less for them over time. Expect a kaleidoscope of consumer electronics products to be available for your entertainment too.

On the Free Way, you can expect to have more freedom to buy, sell, own, keep, use, and donate your private property. An army of social bureaucrats won't stop you at every turn. Your private property will once again be your private property, not subject to the whims of big government.

Rigid and bureaucratic environmental regulations will give way to a more productive and humane way of living in harmony with nature – something Newt Gingrich calls *Green Conservatism*. Limited government will encourage and will provide incentives for *entrepreneurial environmentalists* (again that's Newt Gingrich's term) to use the phenomenal economic efficiency of the free market to accelerate and refine innovative solutions to both environmental challenges and opportunities.

Expect a much better world on the Free Way than the Social Road can ever provide with the command-and-control form of big government. Expect cleaner air to breathe and cleaner water to drink or to use for swimming. Expect both of those things without highly restrictive, environmental laws and regulations.

On the Free Way, expect that your energy supplies will increase and your energy costs will decline as foolish energy regulations are relaxed. America's energy resources are abundant. Instead of $7.00 per gallon gasoline in a year or two, think of gasoline that costs $1.50 per gallon in two years. Instead of brownouts and energy shortages in the near future, think of abundant electric power at lower rates than today.

In fact, American energy supplies far exceed our needs. There is no economic reason that we need to hand over so much of our money to foreign energy suppliers. Plus, importantly, we can utilize our energy resources to meet our own needs in America without doing vast damage to our environment that many, radical environmentalists fear will take place.

With regard to the so-called global warming crisis, all Americans need to rely on solid scientific research that is not based on political consensus or politically-motivated programs and policies. Progressives and socialists have had the most to gain from stirring up the global warming fears that have given children bad dreams at night and have tied the fate of the planet to our turning over control of energy to big government.

On the Free Way, expect to return to non-emotional-based science that looks at evidence, verifies experimental data, and cautiously debates conclusions, which are always tentative and subject to new theories and new empirical evidence. That's how real science works. Scientists don't jump to political conclusions, freeze all debate, and settle into never-ending "consensus." Maybe, that's how "progressive science" functions, but it's certainly not how real science that seeks to discover the truth about the physical world really works.

Indeed, America and the world have seen too much junk science, too many scares, too many artificially-generated "crises," in recent years which conveniently help push us down the Social Road.

On the Free Way, intellectual freedom demands intellectual honesty. On the Free Way, data trumps emotions and political consensus.

To sum up, the Free Way truly provides a better lifestyle and a significantly higher standard of living for you and your family with economic freedom, economic growth, and limited government.

Now that we have taken a look at the impact of the Free Way on your lifestyle, let's think about its impact on your health.

The Free Way and Your Health

The Free Way not only offers a richer, more rewarding lifestyle, but it also provides a healthier lifestyle for you too. Why? Well, for one thing, big government is not involved on the Free Way. If you study any big government on the Social Road that provides socialized medicine to its poor citizens, you find such things as, shortages, rationing, waiting lines, high costs, low benefits, and patients that suffer and die for lack of adequate health care.

On the Free Way, health care is an industry that seeks to grow and improve. On the Social Road, health care is another big government agency or set of departments that seek to ration its services and cut its costs.

On the Free Way, patients are free to pick their own doctors (and doctors don't stop practicing because of big government regulations and low pay). On the Free Way, doctors focus on their patient's health care (not on what big government allows them to do). On the Free Way, doctors work for patients. They don't work for big government.

On the Free Way, costs are contained or drop, because of competition in the Free Market and through innovation. Consider a quick example. In America's health care industry, in the recent past, there were only two industry segments that had costs go down – laser eye surgery and cosmetic surgery. All other segments saw increasing prices. Just think. Laser eye surgery and cosmetic surgery were the only two health care industry segments that were NOT regulated by big government. Without big government regulation, their costs went down.

In the debate before the 2010 health care bill became law, progressives complained that the health care system was broken. That was true. What they failed to point out was that big government was the reason why the system was broken. At the time, about 50% of the health care industry was controlled directly by big government through various tax and regulatory policies. In addition, most of the rest of the health care industry was indirectly controlled by big government. Big government was the problem.

Instead of returning to a free market in health care which would have brought down health care costs and health insurance costs, big government chose to double-down on socialism. If not repealed or ruled unconstitutional, that will prove to be a major mistake – from both a health care perspective and an economic perspective. On the Social Road, the quality of health care declines.

In contrast, on the Free Way, the quality of health care improves steadily. The free market provides incentives to patients to find the most cost-effective health care providers, tests, procedures, therapies, and drugs. The free market also provides doctors, hospitals, medical device companies, drug companies, and entrepreneurs with incentives to innovate, diagnose more accurately, treat more quickly, and raise quality across the entire health care industry. There are additionally market incentives to cut costs, while maintaining or improving existing quality, throughout the industry.

On the Free Way, health care insurance companies are free to innovate with new, better policies that target the needs of various market segments. One-size-fits-all policies don't make sense in a nation with over 300,000,000 potential customers. Innovative health care insurance products would drive down health care insurance costs considerably.

On the Free Way, expect your health care to be better than on the Social Road and your health care quality to be the best in the world. The free market works marvelously well.

The Free Way to the Good Life

As you can see, the Free Way leads to economic growth and prosperity. It also leads to peace and harmony among nations. It is the path to the Good Life.

The Free Way is all about freedom – religious freedom, political freedom, economic freedom, and intellectual freedom – and how these freedoms are inextricably linked together to help create economic growth, prosperity, and peace.

The Free Way means freedom and limited government that protects the nation from external threats (such as war and terrorism) and protects the nation from internal threats (such as violence and crime). The Free Way means lots of job opportunities and a job for everyone that wants to work. The Free Way means lower taxes on economic growth, fewer burdensome regulations, a stronger economy, a brighter future, and more money in your checking account. The Free Way means both a better lifestyle and a higher standard of living. The Free Way means better health care.

The Free Way is the path to the Good Life.

Chapter 3

The Freeway to the Good Life

"For you were called to freedom, brethren; only do not use
your freedom as an opportunity for the flesh,
but through love be servants of one another."
Galatians 5:13

If you agree that the Free Way is a much better economic vision than the Social Road, you face perhaps the most important question an American citizen can ever ask. What must America do to live on the Free Way? Or, put in a slightly different manner. What must America do to be free, prosperous, and peaceful?

Fortunately, America's Founding Fathers put together a marvelous document called The Constitution of the United States of America that serves as a framework for assuring America is free, prosperous, and peaceful. To that wonderful document, we need only add some practical knowledge from the field of economics.

This chapter summarizes the Freeway to the Good Life – the Constitutional framework plus a pro-growth economic roadmap to achieve, maintain, and grow the economic vision of the Free Way. It's a reasonably simple and direct route to assure America is free, prosperous, and peaceful.

Let's start by looking at the Constitutional framework on the Freeway to the Good Life.

The Constitutional Framework

America is an exceptional nation. It was founded on two exceptional documents. First, The Declaration of Independence was vitally important to America's founding because it established a moral vision for what a legitimate government should be. Then, it resolutely declared the political bonds between the United Colonies and the British Crown to be dissolved and the United States of America to be Free and Independent

States. Second, the Constitution was crucial to America's founding because it established a political vision and a pragmatic framework for a limited government that protects our freedoms. The Founding Fathers believed in limited government whose power came from the people and whose primary purpose was the protection of the liberties of its citizens.

The Constitution enables the Free Way and is incompatible with the Social Road. That's why there is so much animosity among conservatives and progressives today. That's the essence of America's Economic War that I wrote about in my book *America's Economic War – Your Freedom, Money and Life.*

What are the key elements of the Constitutional framework on the Freeway to the Good Life?

>>> First Amendment – Freedom of Religion, Freedom of Religious Expression, and Freedom of Speech

Freedom starts with Freedom of Religion and Freedom of Religious Expression. Both are protected by the First Amendment to the Constitution. Both have been under heavy assault by progressives who seek to eliminate religion from the Public Square and who seek to limit or eliminate your religious freedom. The reasons why go beyond the scope of this book, but are presented clearly and concisely in my book, *America's Economic War.*

The Constitution does not outlaw religion or religious expression. Instead, it protects both. The separation of church and state is a much misunderstood and misinterpreted concept used to drag people down the Social Road. Don't be misled.

The Good Life is impossible without morality and the positive impact of religion on culture and civilization. Freedom is not possible without morality as well. Plus, our Christian and Jewish heritage opens us up to the concepts of human dignity and human compassion, not found in atheistic and secular philosophies. Importantly, the moral vision for The Declaration of Independence comes from our religious heritage as well.

The Good Life also requires Freedom of Speech. As was mentioned earlier in this book, politically correct speech, "hate speech," the "Fairness Doctrine," Net Neutrality (aka "Web Fairness Doctrine"), campaign finance reform, and stifling academic freedom on campuses – all are attempts by proponents of the Social Road to limit or eliminate Freedom of Speech.

To achieve the Good Life, we need to protect our First Amendment freedoms.

>>> Second Amendment – Freedom to Keep and Bear Arms

Freedom, the Good Life, and even sometimes just simply personal safety and a sense of personal security require the Freedom to Keep and Bear Arms.

To achieve the Good Life, we need to protect our Second Amendment freedom.

>>> Ninth Amendment, Fourteenth Amendment, and the Presumption of Liberty

The Ninth Amendment to the Constitution provides a powerful protection of liberty to American citizens. It states:

The enumeration in the Constitution, of certain rights, shall not be construed to deny or disparage others retained by the people.

By itself, the Ninth Amendment guarantees American citizens a broad range of liberties. Taken together with the Privileges and Immunities Clause of the Fourteenth Amendment that reads:

No State shall make or enforce any law which shall abridge the privileges or immunities of citizens of the United States ...

the Constitution can reasonably be interpreted to set up a *Presumption of Liberty* for any liberty that the Federal government might want to restrict. For readers who want to delve into a more sophisticated and detailed legal analysis of the Constitution on this topic, Randy E. Barnett's book, *Restoring the Lost Constitution: The Presumption of*

Liberty, is one place to start your study.

While it's true that the Ninth Amendment has largely been ignored over the years, it nonetheless still exists to protect the liberties of American citizens.

>>> Tenth Amendment and the Right of States to Nullify Unconstitutional Federal Laws

The Tenth Amendment to the Constitution is closely related to the Ninth Amendment. It states:

The powers not delegated to the United States by the Constitution, nor prohibited by it to the States, are reserved to the States respectively, or to the people.

The impact of the Tenth Amendment is to put a further check on the powers of the Federal government. The reasoning is straight forward. Since the Constitution was originally an agreement among the States, the Federal government was merely the result of an agreement by the States. That is, the States preceded the Federal government; the States created the Federal government with the Constitution; and hence, the States were superior to the Federal government.

That's why if the Federal government ever created a law that was inconsistent with the Constitution, the States (or even any one State) could nullify that unconstitutional law, declaring it to be null and void and of no force. The reason why just one State can nullify an unconstitutional law by itself is simple. It's a result of the fact that each State is an equal party to the original agreement, the Constitution, with no one State being superior to any other State.

In effect with the Tenth Amendment, the Founding Fathers placed another protective wall between the liberties of the people and any potential future attempt by the Federal government to gain unbridled power over the people. Indeed, Thomas Jefferson felt so strongly about the Tenth Amendment that he believed it was the most critical component of the Constitution.

It's vitally important for justices and judges to recognize and utilize the

Tenth Amendment in its legal reasoning and in its subsequent decisions.

Incidentally, both the Ninth and Tenth Amendments might turn out to play a pivotal role in declaring the 2010 health care law unconstitutional.

>>> Article 1 – Freedom of Economic Activity (Economic Freedom)

The protection of economic freedom, or the Freedom of Economic Activity, is an integral part of the Constitution. That's why a number of Articles and Amendments touch on it, either directly or indirectly.

Below are some of the places in the Constitution that deal with the Freedom of Economic Activity. They are also some of the most flagrantly attacked and blatantly misinterpreted by progressives who seek to have us go down the Social Road that ultimately leads to economic bankruptcy.

Article 1 Section 8 has three important clauses – Clause 1, the General Welfare Clause (sometimes referred to as the Spending Clause); Clause 3 – the Commerce Clause; and Clause 18, the Necessary and Proper Clause. While it goes beyond the scope of this book to go into detail on these clauses, it's worth noting that Article 1 Section 8 protects economic freedom in areas related to private property rights.

Article 1 Section 10 deals with upholding voluntary contracts. It's vital for all parties to a contract to know that government will hold parties accountable for the contracts they have signed. Contracts build the trust necessary for economic activity to take place in a free market. In a number of cases, this Section has been virtually gutted. Its purpose is to support economic freedom among freely acting parties.

These Article 1 clauses, often weakened by progressive court decisions, need to be read by justices and judges as the Founding Fathers originally intended in order to strengthen and protect our economic freedom.

>>> Fifth Amendment – Freedom of Economic Activity (Economic Freedom)

The Fifth Amendment is a significant protection for private property rights and economic freedom too. As mentioned earlier in this book, the Fifth Amendment states that:

No person shall ... be deprived of life, liberty, or property, without due process of law; nor shall private property be taken for public use, without just compensation.

The Fifth Amendment clearly limits eminent domain – the taking of private property by the government. But, the power of eminent domain has been expanded far beyond the original intent of the Constitution to include such things as *regulatory takings,* that regulate if and how private property can be used and thereby limit or lower the value of private property without just compensation. It has also been used to seize private property for use by other private parties in the name of "economic development" and has been used in *civil asset forfeiture* cases as well. Designating private property as "blighted" is still another means for big government-controlled "economic development."

Once again, the Constitution needs to be interpreted by justices and judges as the Founding Fathers originally intended, if we want to keep our economic freedom and stay on the Freeway to the Good Life.

Our Constitutional framework is one part of the Freeway to the Good Life. Let's look at the second part next – a pro-growth economic roadmap.

Pro-Growth Economic Roadmap

Thanks to a lot of good economists over the years, we understand pro-growth economics fairly well. We know what works. We know what doesn't work. Here are the types of fiscal and monetary policies that America needs today to get us out of the Great Recession before it turns into the Great Double-Dip Recession or worse, before it deteriorates into the Second Great Depression.

> > > Taxes

Taxes are an economic disincentive. In general, when you tax something, you tend to get less of it. In effect, it raises the price or the cost of the item. Same thing happens with the economy. If you tax economic growth, you get less of it. To spur and encourage economic growth, taxes need to be lowered or eliminated on income, savings, and investment. Here's the high level outline for taxes in one potential economic growth plan.

- Personal Income – Taxed at a flat rate of 15% above a threshold of $50,000 of income.
- Corporate Income – Taxed at a flat rate of 15%.
- Capital Gains – Taxes are eliminated. No Tax.
- Death (Estate) Taxes – Taxes are eliminated. No Tax.
- Gift Taxes – Taxes are eliminated. No Tax.

This type of tax plan would generate enormous growth and still bring in substantial revenues to the government. There are a variety of ways deductions can be vastly simplified too. In addition, there are supporting pro-growth changes to the tax code that can be made.

Under pro-growth economic policies, expect unemployment to drop considerably, probably to about 4% to 5% or even lower, in a relatively short period of time (estimated to take approximately two years). Also, you can anticipate GDP growth to accelerate to estimated, sustained levels in the 4% to 6% range as part of a robust economic recovery.

Arthur B. Laffer and Stephen Moore, in their book *Return to Prosperity: How America Can Regain Its Economic Superpower Status,* offer a comprehensive discussion of taxes and tax policy. If you want to consider more ideas on tax policy, it is one place you can start.

>>> Spending

High levels of spending by big government lead to enormous deficits and unsustainable debt levels for America. We need to cut reckless, big government spending. Here's one straight forward plan for cutting big government spending.

- Cut $200 Billion from the Federal budget for the next fiscal year.
- Cut $200 Billion from the Federal budget additionally each fiscal year until the Federal budget is balanced.
- Optional – Consider some form of a Balanced Budget Amendment to the Constitution that requires the Federal government to live on a balanced budget, except in the cases of declared war or a declared national emergency. This idea has merit; but, the wording and

implementation of such a potential amendment might prove challenging.

This approach to spending might be called *no free lunch budgeting*. It's the realization that a big government can't increase spending, taxes, and borrowing indefinitely and expect a healthy, robust economy. A potential Balanced Budget Amendment might also be called the "Let's Not Saddle Our Children with High Debt Amendment."

>>> Regulations

Excessive regulations and big government involvement in free markets is an economic roadmap for decline, not growth. Here's one policy plan for helping to boost the economy quickly and for building a strong foundation for long-term economic growth:

- Deregulate the Health Care Industry and the Health Care Insurance Industry.
- Deregulate the Financial Industry.
- Deregulate the Energy Industry.

The causes of many, if not most, of the major challenges America has faced in recent years with health care, health care insurance, the financial industry, energy costs, and energy independence can all be traced back to big government regulations, mandates, and tax policies that hinder, hamper, and handicap the market in each of these industries.

We can have lower cost and higher quality health care and health care insurance, if big government gets out of the way.

We can have lower costs and a better financial industry, if big government gets out of the way. We can let big companies that mismanage their businesses fail, rather than bail them out. The possibility of bankruptcy without bailouts is a strong motivation for executives to manage prudently. What CEO would want to have a major bankruptcy on their resume?

Plus, we can have lower energy costs and more abundant energy supplies, if big government gets out of the way. America has abundant energy resources that can be utilized in efficient and environmentally-friendly ways. America can also be energy independent, if it chooses to be. Why not let Americans have abundant and affordable energy while preserving our environment?

>>> Monetary Policy

A key component of any policy plan to foster economic growth is to have a monetary policy that emphasizes a strong dollar and moderate money supply growth on a par with the growth of the economy. This leads to low inflation and modest interest rates. These policy choices will help create economic growth and prosperity. In contrast, easy money and a weak dollar, high inflation, and close-to-zero interest rates are not the economic policies to follow for sustained, healthy economic growth. Here's a suggested monetary policy plan for economic growth.

- Follow a strong dollar policy.
- Follow a moderate money supply growth policy.
- Stay focused on low inflation.
- Stay focused on moderate interest rates.

Together our Constitutional framework and a pro-growth economic roadmap make up the Freeway to the Good Life.

Summary

As an American citizen, you are powerful. You a participant in designing and building the 21st century. What's your vision for America? What will it look like? How beautiful will the design be? Will we all have freedom and prosperity? Will nations finally achieve peace throughout the world?

Your individual choice to go down the Social Road or the Free Way is up to you. Of course, your individual choice, when combined with all American citizens, will help to influence and determine the future of America and the world. As an American citizen, you play a crucial role in building America's future.

The economic vision of the Free Way is a superior economic vision to the Social Road. The Free Way leads to economic growth, prosperity, and peace. In stark contrast, the Social Road always leads to moral and economic bankruptcy.

To achieve, maintain, and grow the economic vision of the Free Way, we need to stay on the Freeway to the Good Life – using our Constitutional framework of religious freedom, political freedom, and economic freedom; and using a pro-growth economic roadmap of sensible fiscal and monetary policies.

Today, at the beginning of the 21st century, each economic vision is competing for your mind and fighting for your support. Your choice of economic visions will help to determine whether America and our civilization will grow or decline; whether we will live in prosperity or struggle with poverty; and whether we will live in peace or at war. You have enormous power as a citizen to influence, shape and decide America's future. Truly, your choice and the choices of millions of other citizens will ultimately impact and help to determine which economic vision will become reality in America and in the world.

America's greatest days are ahead of us – with faith, freedom, and free markets – on the Freeway to the Good Life.

God Bless America.

www.ingramcontent.com/pod-product-compliance
Lightning Source LLC
Chambersburg PA
CBHW051244170526
45165CB00004B/1569